3-D THRILLERS!

SEA MONSTERS

PAUL HARRISON

Capella

WHAT IS A SEA

L egends of sea monsters have been told for as long as people have spent their evenings swapping stories. Seafarers have always come back with terrifying tales of mysterious creatures. There must be something about being at the mercy of the waves that messes with the mind — or is there something more to these unlikely myths?

TO BOLDLY GO

What we have to remember is that sailing could be a terrifying experience. Battling stormy seas in leaky wooden boats was a constant reminder of how close a neighbour death could be. Explorers pushed the boundaries of the known world further and further, and with this came a natural fear of the unknown — and being lost and exhausted is bound to cause havoc with your nerves!

MONSTER?

STRANGE WORLD

Not all the blame for these tall tales lies with sailors, though. People who regularly took to the sea were used to seeing such creatures as whales or sharks – but they tended not to be the people who could write. The passengers tended to be the literate ones, as they could afford education and travel, often at sea for the only time in their lives. Imagine seeing a whale for the first time and not knowing what it was – you would probably think that you had seen a monster, too! Other scholars who wrote of sea monsters may not even have been to sea themselves at all, but were merely recounting tales that had been told to them.

SCARE STORIES

Sometimes, stories of sea monsters were not just used for entertainment. Some early traders deliberately spread rumours of sea monsters as a way of scaring off the competition from following their highly profitable trade routes. Why bother going all the way to a distant port when there was a good chance you'd end up as a light lunch for a creature from the deep?

Many old sea maps are covered with pictures of monsters, partly as decoration, partly as warnings and to symbolize danger and the unknown.

DEM BONES

In the past, superstition was rife. Not everything has a simple explanation, so the supernatural replaced most things which today can be accounted for by science. Dinosaur bones on land helped fuel the belief in dragons – so why shouldn't monsters live in the sea, too? Such beliefs were bolstered when rotting carcasses of whales or other large marine life were washed onto the shore. The decayed corpses looked like nothing anyone had ever seen, and were consequently rumoured to be monsters.

ANCIENT MON

Life developed in the seas long before it did on land, so it'll come as no surprise that there have been some pretty scary creatures floating around our oceans in the past. The top predators on the planet used to live in the water — and here are some of the most impressive.

Sharks first appeared on earth around 400 million years ago.

SNAP, SNAP!

One type of ancient sea monster which is still with us today is the crocodile. The largest crocodile today — the estuarine, or saltwater, crocodile — grows over 6 metres in length. This is impressive enough, but it's positively tiny compared to its ancient relatives. Some early forms of crocodile were absolutely huge — up to 12 metres long!

TERS

TOOTHLESS TERROR

Over 360 million years ago, one fish not to be messed with was Dunkleosteus (dun-klee-OS-tee-us). At around 5.5 metres long, this armour-plated monster was bigger than today's great white shark. Although Dunkleosteus didn't have teeth – each jaw had a hard bony edge instead – it was still the top predator of the day and was more than happy to eat anything which crossed its path.

MESOZOIC MAULER

One of the most fearsome creatures ever to roam the oceans was the Liopleurodon (LIE-o-PLOOR-o-don). It terrorized the seas during the Mesozoic era, around 150 million years ago. At around 15 metres in length, and with a ferocious reputation to match, it was more than big enough to be a worry to everything else in the ocean, and even unwary dinosaurs paddling along the shore.

NESSIE

Of course, one of the most famous monsters in the world is Nessie – rumoured to inhabit Loch Ness in Scotland. Like many other lake monsters around the world, it is thought that Nessie is a living plesiosaur (plez-ee-o-saw) – a marine reptile from the time of the dinosaurs. Nessie-spotters often claim to have seen a long neck and a hump-back, which is just what a plesiosaur looked like. Could this mean some ancient reptiles still exist?

SEA SERPENTS

The classic sea monster is, of course, the sea serpent. There have been reports of gigantic snake-like terrors in the oceans for hundreds of years, but what's the real story behind this particular menace?

STATESIDE SERPENT

Chesapeake Bay, off the east coast of America, is reputedly home to a large sea serpent nicknamed Chessie. In 1982, a Chesapeake resident named Robert Frew spotted Chessie and managed to capture it – on video tape, that is. The tape went off to the Smithsonian Institute to be examined but, unfortunately, the quality was too poor for scientists to say exactly what it was that Frew saw. So is Chessie real, or is it really something more mundane – a seal or a manatee perhaps?

INLAND SERPENTS

You may not even have to go to sea to spot monstrous serpents – some people believe that some lakes are home to their own monsters. The most famous lake monsters are Nessie from Loch Ness in Scotland, Ogopogo from Lake Okanagan in British Columbia, Canada, and Champ from Lake Champlain in the USA. It has been claimed that these lakes may have underground passages to the ocean, allowing the monsters to meet other sea monsters and breed.

In 1840, the crew of the ship Pekin were convinced they spotted a sea monster. It turned out to be a big lump of seaweed. Could this be another explanation for sightings of monsters too?

FABULOUS FISH

One thing is beyond doubt – one kind of sea serpent does exist. Don't believe it? Well then check out exhibit A, the oarfish. At around 9 metres long, and with a red dorsal fin running the length of its body, the oarfish looks quite unlike any other species of fish. Could this unusual beast be what sailors have been spotting for all these years?

SNAKES ALIVE

Of course, there are actually snakes which swim in the sea too. Some of these sea snakes have flattened bodies which help them to swim, and also make them look more odd than they really are. And could reports of the river dwelling anaconda of South America – which grows over 9 metres in length – have convinced some people that such monsters live in the ocean too?

SUCKERED IN

T ake a peek at an octopus or a squid — it has looks only a mother could love. That rubbery texture and all those suckery legs writhing around like a nest of snakes is enough to give many people nightmares. Imagine how you would feel seeing a gigantic version of one of those bearing down on you if you were out for a paddle.

There's plenty of evidence of really big squid – sperm whales are often found with huge sucker marks on their skin from fights with these massive creatures.

KRAKEN

The most notorious of the ancient, squid-like monsters was the Kraken, and there have been many tales of this giant creature rearing out of the sea and dragging boats down beneath the waves with them. It was claimed, in the 1700s – by the Bishop of Bergen no less, so you'd hope he was telling the truth – that the Kraken was as big as an island. Now that would make a scary holiday destination!

Seafarers have long told tales of giant octopus and squid attacking their ships. It's such a well-worn theme that these episodes have made it into literature, too – most famously H. G. Wells' *Twenty Thousand Leagues Under the Sea*. Of course, there's little reliable documentary evidence that such attacks ever occurred, but that doesn't mean such monsters don't exist.

GIANT OCTOPUS

Lusca is the name given to a type of giant octopus that is meant to live in the Caribbean. Legend has it that these monsters are around 40 metres long – around ten times bigger than the documented size for giant octopi. There's little proof that Luscas exist, of course, but a series of old photographs showing a mysterious body washed up in the Bahamas might suggest they are out there...

REAL-LIFE MONSTER

Today, the closest thing we know of to the Kraken is the giant squid. Some scientists estimate that it could grow up to around 13 metres long – that's about the length of a bus. There is some evidence, however, of a colossal squid that could possibly be twice the size of the giant squid – that's a lot of calamari!

The fear sailors had of sea monsters was two-fold. Firstly, the monster might sink the ship, leaving the sailors either to drown or be cast adrift to a slow death. Secondly, it might have a taste for a sailor-snack and eat them. But how likely is it that a person could get eaten at sea?

The throats and stomachs of most whales and sharks are too small to swallow a human.

DEADLY TASTER

Of course, sailors may well have seen people eaten by some types of shark. Undoubtedly, sharks like the great white and tiger shark have and do eat people, but actually humans aren't their favourite food. Most attacks are actually the shark having a quick taster, only to leave the victim alone realizing that it's not the type of snack they're after.

HOLE

THE LEGEND OF JONAH

The idea of being swallowed by a sea monster is ingrained in myths, legends and even religion. The bible tells a story of a man called Jonah who was swallowed by a large fish. After he prayed to God, the fish let him go.

BIG FISH

Would it be possible to be eaten by a basking or whale shark? After all, they are the two biggest types of fish in the sea (remember, whales are mammals). However, like many whales, these two sharks eat tiny sea creatures and aren't likely to swallow something as big as a man.

TINY FOOD

Whales certainly look big enough to eat a person, and they are the biggest animals in the sea. However, many whales eat tiny sea creatures called krill which they trap in comb-like plates of bone in their mouth called baleen. It's difficult to imagine that a baleen whale would want to – or could – eat a human. Other whales have teeth, and the biggest of these is the sperm whale. Interestingly, there is a tale that a sailor called James Bartley was swallowed alive by a sperm whale during the 1890s and survived for 16 hours in the whale's stomach!

A s we have seen, not all sea monsters are figments of people's imaginations. In truth, the oceans are home to some of the strangest animals you could imagine — and some of the very oddest are found at the very bottom of the sea.

LURING THEM IN

The bottom of the ocean is so far from the surface that even sunlight can't get down all that way. Instead, sea creatures here produce their own light. The aptly named anglerfish uses a glowing ball of light hanging from its dorsal fin to attract small fish, like an angler with a baited hook. When the fish get too close, the anglerfish suddenly springs to life and gulps the hapless victim down.

FANG-TASTIC

Some of the scariest teeth to be found in the ocean belong to the viperfish – they're so big they can't even fit inside the fish's mouth. Fortunately, the fish is only 25 cm long, so it's not a real threat to anything on the large side.

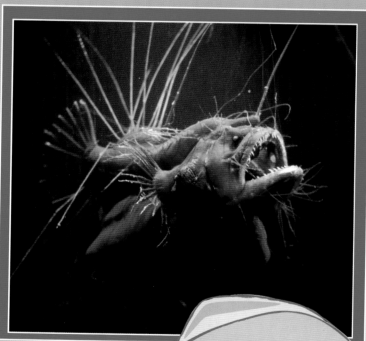

Some scientists believe that up to 90 percent of deep sea fish can produce their own light.

BIG MOUTH

The gulper eel has two of the biggest advantages for a deep sea predator – a huge mouth and an expanding stomach. The gulper eel's already large mouth can actually unhinge, or dislocate, allowing it to swallow prey as big as itself. Fortunately, its stomach can stretch just as much to accommodate the eel's sizeable lunch.

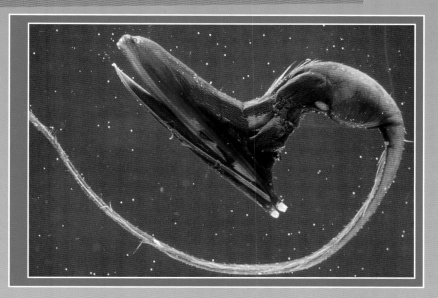

JEEPERS CREEPERS

The Greenland shark's shining eyes make it look more menacing than it really is – actually it's quite a harmless creature. This rare shark is one of the few which live in arctic waters, where it can be found in both deep and shallow water, depending on the time of year. It is also one of the largest sharks alive. The light in its eyes is not produced by the fish itself, but by a parasite which lives on the poor shark's peepers.

The only way to tell for sure whether there are sea monsters out there is to find them. Unfortunately, that's easier said than done. There's a lot of water out there — it covers over 70 percent of the planet — and these sea creatures can be very elusive.

Cryptids is what cryptozoologists call the mysterious monsters they look for.

MEGA SURPRISE

What we can be fairly sure about is that there will probably be big animals out there that we don't know about. And finding them seems to be a matter of luck. Until 1976, no one knew that the megamouth shark ever existed, and then one got caught accidentally by a research vessel. If something as big as this 5 metre shark can stay hidden for all this time, perhaps, just perhaps, there really are some big monsters out there waiting to be found.

BEACHCOMBING

Sometimes scientists don't have to go looking for interesting creatures. Instead, the sea washes them up, or fishermen net them by mistake. Generally, these creatures have been dead for a long time and are badly decomposed. In 1977, a Japanese trawler hauled what look like a dead plesiosaur from the waves. There was great excitement until scientists pointed out that this is exactly what basking sharks look like as they rot.

SCIENTISTS OR NUTTERS?

The practice of looking for animals that most people consider to be either myths or extinct is called cryptozoology. Many people pour scorn on cryptozoologists, declaring them not to be proper scientists. However, some cryptozoologists do use very strict scientific criteria in their work.

HIDE AND SEEK

Most of the sea remains unexplored, mainly because it's quite difficult to study such a large area properly. Also, the sea bed isn't nice and flat, instead it's made up of mountains and trenches – some more than 11 kilometres deep – so there are plenty of places for creatures to hide.

This edition published in 2006 by Arcturus Publishing Limited
26/27 Bickels Yard, 151–153 Bermondsey Street,
London SE1 3HA

In Canada published for Indigo Books
468 King St W, Suite 500,
Toronto, Ontario M5V 1L8

Author: Paul Harrison
Designer: Talking Design, Maki Ryan, Beatriz Waller

Cover design: Maki Ryan, Beatriz Waller
Editor: Rebecca Gerlings
Illustrator (glasses): Ian Thompson

Picture credits:
NHPA: front cover; page 4; page 11, bottom; page 13, top; page 15,
bottom.
Nature Picture Library: page 7, bottom; page 9, bottom;
page 10; page 12, top and bottom; page 15.
Science Photo Library: title page; page 3, bottom; page 6; page 9, top;
page 11, middle and back cover; page 15, top; page 16.
Natural History Museum: page 5, top and bottom.
Topfoto: page 3, top; page 6, top; page 8; page 11, top.
Bridgeman Art Library: page 2.
Chris Harvey-Clark: page 13.

3-D images by Pinsharp 3D Graphics

Printed in China

ISBN-13: 978-1-84193-392-4
ISBN-10: 1-84193-392-9